MAZETTI *Choklad*

Let's visit
SWEDEN

D.E. GOULD

BURKE

First published July 1976
Second revised edition 1984
© Dennis E. Gould 1976 and 1984

ACKNOWLEDGEMENTS

The authors and publishers are grateful to the following individuals and organisations for permission to reproduce photographs in this book:
Ervaco; International Photobank; Reportgebild; SAS; The Swedish Institute; The Swedish National Tourist Office; The Swedish Tourist Traffic Association; Tiofoto; United Nations Association of Sweden.

CIP data
Gould, Dennis E.
    Let's visit Sweden – 2nd ed.
    1.   Sweden – Social life and customs – Juvenile literature
    I.   Title
    948.5'05   DL631
    ISBN 0 222 01032 0

Burke Publishing Company Limited
Pegasus House, 116-120 Golden Lane, London EC1Y 0TL, England.
Burke Publishing (Canada) Limited
Registered Office: 20 Queen Street West, Suite 3000, Box 30, Toronto, Canada M5H 1V5.
Burke Publishing Company Inc.
Registered Office: 333 State Street, PO Box 1740, Bridgeport, Connecticut 06601, U.S.A.
Filmset in "Monophoto" Baskerville by Green Gates Studios Ltd., Hull, England.
Printed in Singapore by Tien Wah Press (Pte) Ltd.

Contents

SWEDEN

NARVIK

Kiruna

Kebnekaise
2117

ARCTIC CIRCLE

LULEÅ

Lapland

UMEÅ

Norrland

GULF OF BOTHNIA

NORWAY

SCANDINAVIAN MOUNTAIN RANGE

FINLAND

MORA

Dalarna

FALUN

ÅLAND

Svealand

UPPSALA

L. Mälaren

STOCKHOLM

L. Vänern

GÖTEBORG

Götaland

Visby

SEA

GOTLAND

Orrefors

DENMARK

Skåne

ÖLAND

KALMAR

U.S.S.R

LUND

BALTIC

100

200 Miles

COPENHAGEN

MALMÖ

0   100   200   300 Km.

The Land and the People

Sweden is the fourth largest country in Europe, and stretches between latitudes 55° and 69° north. The most southerly part lies in the same latitudes as the border between England and Scotland. Sweden is 1,574 kilometres (nearly 1,000 miles) long, from the southern tip to the extreme northern regions; and these northern regions extend for approximately 320 kilometres (over two hundred miles) inside the Arctic Circle. The surface area of the land is about twice that of the United Kingdom.

Stamp-collectors know that the word SVERIGE appears on most stamps from Sweden. It is pronounced something like *svair-i-yer*, and means "the kingdom of the Svear". The Goths and the Svear were among the tribes of people who lived in

An ore train, bringing ore from the Arctic region of Sweden to the harbour

this part of Northern Europe over a thousand years ago. To this day the country is divided into three parts: Götaland (Land of the Goths) in the south, Svealand (Land of the Svear) in the middle, and Norrland in the north. These divisions play no practical part at all in the life of the country, although they are often mentioned in weather reports and forecasts. For the purpose of administration, Sweden is divided into districts, called *län*. However, the older divisions are of greater historical interest and are more commonly used in general conversation when referring to different parts of Sweden.

The Swedish language belongs to the same group as English and German. Swedes can read Norwegian and Danish without very much difficulty. Understanding each other's spoken language is not quite so easy, but people from these Scandinavian countries can usually make themselves understood to one another without great difficulty.

Sweden, Norway and Denmark, together with Finland and Iceland, form a group of nations known as the Nordic countries. They are very keen to co-operate, and they work together as closely as possible. Sweden is the largest of the Nordic countries, in both area and population.

Norway lies to the west of Sweden, and the countries are divided by a long boundary through the Scandinavian Mountain Range, also called Kölen ("Keel"). These two countries together form the Scandinavian Peninsula. A short boundary in the north-east, through barren and sparsely populated regions, separates Sweden from Finland. (The Finnish language is completely different from those of the other Nordic countries, although there is a large area in the south of Finland where Swedish is spoken by over 300,000 people.)

Sweden has no land border with Denmark; a narrow strip of sea separates the two countries. Ferry-boats cross the dividing Sound in about twenty minutes at the narrowest point.

The prevailing wind from the south-west blows over the North Sea and first meets the chains of mountains along the Norwegian-Swedish border. This results in the western side of Sweden receiving the heaviest rainfall. There are tremendous differences in the Swedish climate between the extreme north and south of the country. In the central and southern regions the summer usually lasts for the months of May to August. The long hours of daylight at that time of the year are often combined with long periods of settled weather, and the temperature averages around 20° Celsius (68° Fahrenheit)—though there are often days with the temperature as high as 30°C. (86°F.) The days become noticeably shorter in September and then the autumn tints in the trees are very beautiful. The first frosts usually come in the nights of October and falls of snow are quite common in November, but these seldom settle or last for many days. By Christmas, however, snow and day-time frost are to be expected quite regularly and in normal winters will cover the ground for about three months. The winter day temperatures keep below freezing-point. On really cold days the temperature may go down to −20°C.

(–4°F.) or even –30°C. (–22°F.); but that is not common. The long-awaited spring and the thaw come with a rush. The ground is usually clear by the end of April. Buds and flowers come slowly at first, but in May there is a great burst of growth. With the longer daylight hours flowers blossom quickly, though freedom from frost cannot be taken for granted until the beginning of June.

Much of Sweden is heavily forested, and silver birch trees such as these can be seen throughout the country

The plains of Skåne, Sweden's "granary"

The most southerly province of Sweden is Skåne, also given the latinised name of Scania. In this part of Sweden the crop-growing season may be as long as eight months. In the far north lies Lapland where the growing season may only last for a quarter of the year. However, the very long hours of daylight here during the summer months partly make up for this. For a few weeks around midsummer the sun hardly dips below the horizon. This has earned Sweden the name of "The Land of the Midnight Sun". In these conditions everything grows very rapidly; although crops here *start* to grow very much later, they are finally ready for harvesting only a short time after those grown further south. Figures from the three most northerly administrative districts show that they have the highest potato yield (for their area) in the whole of the country. Strawberries grown on protected valley slopes in Lapland are flown to markets in the south of Sweden.

Mighty rivers rise in the mountainous heights of Sweden and flow down to the Baltic Sea. The north-west regions, which border with Finland, are comparatively flat and in the summer they are swampy. There, in particular during the months of June, July and August, swarms of mosquitoes are a real nuisance which has to be combated.

In the northern regions of Sweden a train journey may last for more than twelve hours without passing through a single town. The train may be forced to stop to avoid the reindeer which wander onto the track. The only signs of civilisation, apart from the telegraph lines and the railway itself, are the occasional clusters of small houses and the tiny villages.

The midnight sun, photographed at twenty-minute intervals between 10.10 p.m. and 12.30 a.m.

A summer cottage in southern Sweden, on the edge of the forest

More than half of the central part of Sweden is covered by forests which form one of the country's main natural resources. It has been jokingly said that the squirrels which thrive in these forests could jump from tree to tree right across the 500 kilometres (310 miles) width of the land. Moose are also quite common in the heavily forested regions. These animals, which have huge antlers, stand about two metres (seven feet) tall, to the shoulder. However, they are not as ferocious as they appear to be, although they are a danger to traffic when they cross the roads as dawn and dusk, to seek their way to water. The moose are protected by law and may only be shot during a certain short hunting period. Sometimes they come out into the open and regularly eat cultivated crops; then special permission may be granted to kill them out of season. Meat from the large carcass of the moose is regarded by many as a delicacy. Further north there are still wild bears, but these are far less common than the protected moose.

In recent years, musk ox have been introduced into the mountainous areas of the provinces of Härjedalen and Jämtland. This experiment seems to be proving successful. These rare, shaggy animals appear to thrive in their new surroundings and the small herds are increasing. Walkers in these mountains are warned to keep a respectful distance away.

Amongst rare animals in Sweden which are increasing in number is the cat-like lynx. The wolf, too, almost became extinct but now attacks on reindeer by wolves have become more frequent once again.

There are many thousands of lakes in Sweden. The numbers claimed by travel agents' brochures vary between 92,000 and 100,000. The three largest are Vänern, Vättern and Mälaren. The former has an area of 5,546 square kilometres (2,143 square miles) and a maximum depth of nearly 100 metres (over 300 feet).

In the very south of the country the landscape is made up of rolling hills and leafy, deciduous forests, mainly of beech and oak. In Skåne (Scania) we find flat, fertile fields with a view over the crops of grain, sugar beet or bright yellow rape (cultivated for its seed from which oil is produced), unbroken by fences or hedges.

There are about eight million people living in Sweden. This is considerably less than the population of London or New York. The average number of inhabitants in Sweden is approximately twenty per square kilometre (fifty per square mile). But for the most northerly third of the country the average figure is very much less.

It is best to be careful when talking about miles in Sweden. The Swedes call ten kilometres a *mil*, which they translate into English as a Swedish mile. So if you are told by a Swede who speaks English that your destination is only a mile away, you may still have quite a way to go!

The characteristic wooden houses to be seen in country districts, painted red with wood preservative which is obtained as a by-product from the copper mines in Falun, are being replaced more and more by large blocks of ultra-modern flats. It is easier, and more economical, to build these flats to withstand the cold winters. The depth to which the frost penetrates the ground demands deep foundations. In most Swedish houses there is, consequently, a very useful cellar area.

Many Swedish families have a second home—a small cottage or cabin, however primitive, where they can enjoy the freedom of the countryside and the various recreational activities to be found there. Their aim seems to be to get right away from other people. Although it is foolish to generalise about a whole nation, it is probably fair to say that the Swedes are a reserved people who do not readily come forward to make the first friendly contacts with a stranger.

It is a common mistake to think of all Swedes as being tall and blond. However, it is true that the majority of Swedes are fair, with light hair and blue, or bluish-grey, eyes. The children, in particular, often have extremely fair hair. But dark hair and

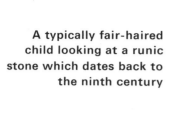

A typically fair-haired child looking at a runic stone which dates back to the ninth century

brown eyes are not at all uncommon among Swedish people.

Before the Second World War very few foreigners lived in Sweden. After the war, however, thousands of refugees and other immigrants sought a new and happier life there; and in the 1960s there was a marked increase in the number of people from southern European countries who travelled to Sweden to find unskilled work. In a few years, Sweden had thus changed from a country with comparatively few foreigners to one where adult immigrants made up about five per cent of the population.

Since 1973, however, immigration has been restricted to citizens of Nordic countries, refugees, people seeking political asylum, relatives and adopted children of Swedish citizens, and skilled labour.

Sweden and her Neighbours through the Ages

About twenty thousand years ago, Northern Europe and large areas of America and Asia were covered by a thick layer of ice. This has been estimated as nearly 1,000 metres (about 3,000 feet) in depth. The effects of this Ice Age are clearly seen in the Swedish landscape. The tremendous pressure of the ice has gouged paths through the granite rock and removed the earth; in other places the glacial rivers resulting from the melting ice have deposited vast plains of fertile soil.

As the climate improved again after the Great Ice Age, vegetation and animal life returned, and eventually human beings settled in parts of Sweden, probably to hunt reindeer and Arctic fox. The oldest human settlement remains discovered in Sweden are estimated as being about 8,000 years old. They are at Sandarna, near Göteborg (Gothenburg).

The first signs of land cultivation and animal farming are from around 3000 B.C. The findings of archeologists have helped to tell the story of the following centuries, through the Bronze Age up to the Iron Age. Many interesting weapons and ornaments have been unearthed.

It was the provinces around Lake Mälaren which became the most important. Uppland, in particular, became a prosperous and powerful part of the country. Rich graves have been discovered in these areas.

The Scandinavians became well-known and feared for their seafaring exploits. The men who carried out these plundering raids across the seas were called Vikings. The main period of their activities was between A.D. 800 and A.D. 1000. The Vikings from those parts which are now called Denmark and Norway tended to concentrate their raids towards the West, whereas those of the Svear were often directed towards lands in the East. They struck across the Baltic Sea and spread as far as the Russian rivers down to the Black Sea and the Caspian Sea. At times their ships had to be hauled overland by men using logs as rollers.

The Swedes established a settlement in Novgorod, which they called Holmgård. In fact the name of Russia is thought by some scholars to be derived from the Swedish name "rus" given to the home area of some of these Viking voyagers.

Riches seized in these raids poured back into Sweden, and these were used, in turn, for trading. A particularly lively trading settlement was at Birka, on an island in Lake Mälaren. This is now a popular tourist attraction near Stockholm.

Stockholm was founded as the capital in A.D. 1250. At that time the population was very largely German. The German cities in the so-called Hanseatic League were extremely powerful trading centres and they had great importance for Sweden's development. This is why so many Germans settled in Sweden. In fact it was necessary to write into the laws of the time that Germans must not form more than half the membership of the town councils. Modern Swedish shows the tremendous influence which these German traders had on the language.

Gustav Vasa, one of
Sweden's most
famous kings

In order to try to control the ever-increasing German domination, the Nordic countries formed a union in 1397. This was known as the Kalmar Union, named after the town on the south-east coast of Sweden where the agreement was drawn up. The Danes grew most powerful in this union and there were continuous quarrels and wars between Denmark and Sweden. King Kristian II of Denmark planned to conquer Sweden and this led to an attack in 1520.

At this time there was no united leadership in Sweden and much treachery amongst the powerful families who sought to rule the land. It was Gustav Vasa who emerged as the saviour of the Swedish people, and the army which he rallied around him successfully drove out the Danes. He led his men into Stockholm on Midsummer's Eve in 1523, having already been crowned King of Sweden on June 6th. This date was celebrated as the Swedish Flag Day until 1983. It is now Swedish National Day. It is the bearded face of Gustav Vasa which appears on the five-kronor Swedish bank-notes. He was a powerful king who reigned for thirty-seven years.

It was Gustav Vasa's grandson, Gustav II Adolf who paved the way to modern Sweden. He is often referred to as Sweden's greatest king. He made his mark in matters of both peace and war. In 1630, Sweden entered into the Thirty Years War, as a result of which large areas of Northern Germany were won. King Gustav was killed in the battle at Lützen, in 1632.

Sweden continued to capture more territory and in 1658 won from Denmark the provinces of Skåne, Halland and Blekinge in the south, and Bohuslän in the west. A spectacular victory was gained when the Swedish army made the risky march across the frozen sea in the straits between Sweden and Denmark, causing the Danes to surrender.

The Period of Greatness, when Sweden was a world-power, eventually came to an end with the death of King Karl XII in 1718. By this time she had lost command of the Baltic countries and many of the German provinces.

Sweden changed during the next hundred years. No longer did the ruler hold supreme power. Instead Sweden had a constitutional government with a strong parliament, called the Riksdag. This was made up of members from amongst the noblemen, clergy, citizens and peasants. Attention was paid to improving conditions at home after all the years of war.

King Gustav III seized power in 1772. For a time the monarch's might was increased once more. But he was still subject to the control of Parliament in many matters, such as taxes and finances. Gustav III was very artistic and particularly interested in the theatre. He did a great deal to encourage the arts, and he helped writers, musicians and playwrights.

The Palace of Drottningholm, just half an hour's drive from the centre of Stockholm, has a great attraction for visitors. The gardens and fountains are set out like the famous ones in Versailles, near Paris. A most remarkable wooden theatre still stands there for which the king wrote plays in which he himself performed. Gustav III was very fond of France and there was a great deal of French influence in the court during his reign. But in spite of the numerous good things which he introduced, there were many who hated him and his frivolous, spendthrift ways. In 1792, he was assassinated at a masked ball, held at the Royal Opera House.

During the reign of Gustav III's son, Sweden became involved in war with Russia and lost Finland.

In 1810, when Sweden found herself without a successor to the throne, a French marshal, Jean Bernadotte, was offered the throne. The present King of Sweden is a descendant of Karl XIV Johan (the Swedish title adopted by the Frenchman). He forced Norway into a union with Sweden. Both

An operatic performance at Drottningholm – the eighteenth-century costumes have great historical value

countries were to have the same king and foreign minister. The constitution was drawn up, however, so that the Norwegian Parliament was free from control by the Swedish king, and Norway eventually became completely independent in 1905.

Karl XIV Johan was a peacemaker. He cultivated friendship with Russia, and Sweden's other neighbours. Neutrality has been Sweden's policy ever since. Attention was turned once more to improvements at home. However, conditions were hard and agricultural production was insufficient for a growing population. During the period from 1860 to 1914, over a million Swedes emigrated, many of them going to North America.

During the years 1918 to 1921 the right to vote became a reality for all men and women in Sweden. A modern multi-party political system came into being and in 1920 the first Labour administration was elected to govern the land.

The Social Democrats have been in power ever since 1936, apart from a short period between 1976 and 1982 when non-socialist coalition governments held power.

23

In 1971 the Swedish Parliament changed from a system of two Houses, an Upper and a Lower, to a Parliament with just one Chamber with 350 members. In 1973 the national elections resulted in 175 seats for the Socialists and 175 for the combined opposition. This most unusual situation resulted in decisions being made by drawing lots when there was an equal result in voting upon matters in Parliament. Steps have been taken to see that such an unsatisfactory situation cannot happen again in the future.

The present King of Sweden is Carl XVI Gustaf. He came to the throne in 1973 at the age of twenty-seven, on the death of his grandfather Gustav VI Adolf. Although there had been much talk about replacing the monarchy by a republic, Gustav VI Adolf was a popular king. He came to the throne at the age of sixty-eight, when most people have already retired. He was thought of by many as an obvious choice for the first Presidency if Sweden did become a republic. However, the

The King and Queen of Sweden, with their three young children

monarchy remains, although the powers of the present young king have been still further reduced by acts of Parliament. Since King Carl XVI Gustaf married Queen Sylvia in 1976, they have had three children and the Royal Family has become a focus for increased popular interest. As from 1980 the successor to the throne will be the first-born, regardless of sex.

Swedish Festivals

Each date in the Swedish calendar is connected with a particular Christian name. Many of the names given to Swedes correspond to those in the calendar, and on that date they celebrate their "name-day". This means that a girl who is christened Rut Elin Inga Lisa has four name-days to be celebrated every year. On each of these days she will probably receive small gifts from her family, and also from friends who would know her name-days, even if they do not know her birthday.

There are many other festivities which are celebrated in Sweden. After the long winter months comes the celebration of the last day of April and the First of May. On the night of April 30th, huge bon-fires are lit and songs of greeting to Spring are sung. It is in the university towns of Uppsala and Lund that these festivities are most gay, but they are also

celebrated throughout the country. In Uppsala, crowds of
students gather on the slopes of the hill leading up to the
University Library. It is traditional that at the stroke of three
o'clock in the afternoon the students remove their dark hats,
which they have been wearing during the months of winter.
Often they throw them into the river Fyris. Then they put on
their white student caps.

Like many Swedish customs, the celebration of the coming
of Spring has its roots in pagan times. Swedish festivities are
often closely connected with the sun and the seasons in this
way. At this time of the year people may be seen in sheltered
corners, sitting with their faces turned to the sun. They are
anxious not to miss a moment of its delightful warmth after
the long cold winter.

Midsummer's day is another occasion for celebrations all

over Sweden. Each community makes a tall Maypole, which is covered with leaves and decorated with flowers. The form of the decorations varies slightly from region to region, but once again there are symbols in the shapes of wreaths of flowers and leaves, which may be traced back to seasonal celebrations in heathen times.

The hoisting of the pole, which may be up to one hundred feet (about thirty metres) tall is accompanied by all kinds of fun and games. Young girls decorate their hair with flowers and the tradition is that if they put the flowers under their pillows that night, then they will dream of their future husband. There is dancing near the Maypole into the small hours of the morning. At this time of the year the northern nights are very short and birds may be heard still singing at midnight.

It is especially at the time of the midsummer festivities that Swedish regional costumes appear, and tourists are particularly attracted to the province of Dalarna (sometimes called Dalecarlia). Many Swedes wear a type of national costume

A Swedish girl in
national costume
with a regional flavour

incorporating the special colour and designs of their own local region. These costumes are very colourful, particularly in Dalarna. The young girls and older women, too, often wear their local costume with its special neckerchief, brooch and hat, showing which village they come from. The men and boys may be seen in hip-length jackets, yellow trousers which reach just below the knees, coloured stockings and buckled shoes. The dancing is led by fiddlers who are also dressed in this costume. Old traditions are kept alive in this way and local pride is widespread.

A very jolly Swedish festivity is the crayfish party. The crayfish is something like a small lobster and is found in many of the Swedish lakes, but the season for catching them is strictly limited by law. It starts on the night of the second Wednesday in August. Men and boys go out onto the lakes in their boats, attract the crayfish with their lanterns, and hope to find a good catch in their pots. They used to be fairly certain of catching crayfish by the score, but now crayfish have become scarce after years of attack by pest. However, many people still hold a crayfish party at the beginning of August. Although the crayfish have been imported, the gay paper serviettes, special paper bibs, table-runners and lanterns brightly decorated with red crayfish keep alive the tradition. Some adults follow the long established custom of drinking snaps, a strong alcoholic drink, after each claw they eat, so that the parties then become very noisy as the guests become more merry. These parties are often held outdoors.

Mårten Gås is celebrated in November. It may be translated as Martin Goose. At this time many Swedish families have a party and eat goose, or perhaps duck instead. This tradition has a religious origin dating back several centuries. When the French bishop, Martin of Tours, was made a saint, the day of his death, November 11th, became a Catholic holy-day. As this coincides with the time of year when the farmers paid their rents and taxes, often in the form of geese or other livestock, the idea of eating goose arose. The Protestant Church also recognised the name of Martin in their celebrations, but the Protestant Martin Goose is on November 10th, the birthday of Martin Luther, the famous German religious reformer.

Advent, the four-week period before Christmas, is widely celebrated in Sweden. In a country where there is otherwise no great evidence of church-going this is rather surprising. Most families put a lighted star in the window at this time. A stand holding four candles is also used during Advent, and this stand may be a piece of beautiful craftmanship in metal or a simple little piece of silver birch log. The candles are lit one by one on each of the four Sundays before Christmas.

Advent is a word which means "the coming" and celebrates the coming of Jesus Christ. The festival of St. Lucia, on December 13th, is not, however, a Christian one and has its roots in pagan times. But, like Advent, it helps to bring light and gaiety into the depth of the Swedish winter. Lucia was the goddess of Light, and the date of her celebration almost coincides with the longest night of the year to be followed by the days getting longer again. In the very far north of Sweden they have three months when they hardly see the sun, although the perpetual snow at that time does help to make life lighter and brighter, and the young people in particular enjoy their winter sports.

On the morning of the St. Lucia celebrations a daughter in the family puts on a long white dress and wears a crown bearing flaming candles. The crown is intertwined with sprigs of evergreen. There were many serious accidents in the past

Celebrating the festival of St. Lucia in the traditional Swedish manner

when girls caught their hair alight. The modern "candles", lit by batteries, are certainly safer although perhaps not quite so pretty. The girl Lucia, is usually attended by young boys who also wear a long white gown and a tall pointed hat which is white and dotted with stars. These are the Star-boys. The little group brings coffee and special Lucia buns to their parents at an early hour in the morning, and may call on the neighbours too.

In the larger towns the festival of St. Lucia has become commercialised and takes the form of a beauty contest. The newspapers present their readers with a selection of beautiful young candidates so that votes may be cast for the St. Lucia of the city for that year.

Christmas is a wonderful time in Sweden. Although it is obviously a Christian festival, there are still connections with the mid-winter festivities which were celebrated in pre-Christian times.

Christmas Eve plays a very important part in the Swedish celebrations. After lunch it is a national holiday. It is during the evening of December 24th that the presents are distributed. The gifts are piled around the foot of the Christmas tree, which is usually as tall as the room will allow. The decorations on the tree often include many Swedish flags, with their yellow cross on a bright blue background. Other decorations include figures and shapes plaited in straw. Among the straw stars and angels there is usually a billy-goat—a reminder of pagan times.

On each present it is customary to write a verse which gives the receiver a clue to the contents of the packet. It is not Father Christmas or Santa Claus who traditionally distributes the presents to the Swedish youngsters, but a little fellow called the "jul-tomte". *Jul* means "yule", and *tomte* is "a little gnome". The young children often put out a bowl of rice-porridge for the jul-tomte. When there are young children in the family someone usually dresses up to play the part.

Even if the snow is a little late coming some years, one can almost guarantee a white Christmas in Sweden. The birds are not forgotten at this time and as the snow and frozen water make it difficult for them to find food, poles with sheaves of corn are put out at Christmas.

In recent years more and more Swedish families have been eating turkey, but the majority still keep to the traditional foods. The main dishes are lut-fisk and rice-porridge. Lut-fisk is a fish which has been dried then soaked in lye, a kind of soda, about three weeks before Christmas. An almond is usually hidden in the rice porridge; it brings luck to the finder, or perhaps indicates that he or she will be the next one to get married.

On Christmas morning the churches are full, although the first service may be as early as five o'clock. In country districts some people still ride to this service in a horse-drawn sledge, with flaming torches lighting their way. And there will certainly be flaming torches outside the church.

One of the Christmas treats for Swedish children is to be

allowed to dip their bread into the gravy made by the large, traditional Christmas Day joint of pork, or maybe even a whole sucking pig. There are usually red tulips to decorate the Christmas table, and in the corner of the room the children will have made a crib. They will probably have helped their mother bake ginger-bread biscuits which are cut out into the shape of stars, Christmas trees or pigs and are often decorated with icing sugar. Some of the ginger-bread mixture will be used to make a ginger-bread house.

December 26th is not celebrated to any great extent, and after about a week the children return to school. On the twentieth day of Christmas there may be a party for the children, when the Christmas tree is ceremoniously stripped of its decorations and taken out of the house.

New Year's Day is a national holiday in Sweden, and there are many parties. The Old Year is rung out by church bells, and fireworks and sparklers are lit to greet the New Year. The period of festivities, which does so much to help break up the winter gloom, is over.

The word "shrove" in Shrove Tuesday comes from a word connected with shriving, which was the process of being beaten in order to show repentance for sins. This was a custom long ago in the Middle Ages. We are reminded of it by the period of Lent in Sweden. It was at this time that people most often would shrive themselves. Nowadays the birch twigs that were once used for beating are gaily decorated with coloured feathers. They are used as indoor decorations

A brilliant display in Stockholm's Haymarket of the coloured feathers used as Spring decorations

at a time when flowers have not yet come into bloom. The numerous stalls selling them in the market places make a delightful splash of colour. After a time indoors the twigs begin to send out green shoots to add to this attractive traditional Spring decoration.

On Easter Saturday, there may come a knock on the front door in Sweden. When you open it you may see a small group of young girls dressed in long, old, colourful clothes, which they have probably borrowed from their mothers or sisters. They have scarves around their heads and their faces are smeared with black. They often carry a copper kettle, and sometimes a broomstick, because they represent the witches from Blåkulla (the Blue Mountain home of witches). They are hoping for small coins, just as some children make carol singing an excuse to do the same. In this way Swedish children keep alive a reminder of the old-time belief in witches, in the Middle Ages.

And so the days lengthen, and Midsummer comes around once more.

Easter witches

Industry, Trade and Transport

A visitor travelling in Sweden, especially in the Central and northern areas, is soon impressed by the rich natural forests and abundant water power, and by the the almost complete lack of large industrial towns. Although many Swedish towns obviously have a great deal of industry going on in them, they do not suffer from the dirt and crowded slums so often found in the built-up areas of other industrial countries.

Sweden also enjoys another rich natural supply which is less obvious since it is under ground—iron ore. The largest deposits of iron ore are in Lapland, in the far north. The ore is unusually rich in the amount of iron which it contains.

There is very little coal to be found in Sweden and there are no significant deposits of oil. Although recent drillings in the island of Gotland, have caused great excitement and raised hopes that Sweden may have her own supplies of oil, the experts see no reason for optimism yet.

Most of Sweden's production has developed in the areas where iron and wood are readily available. In an extensive country with a comparatively small population, vast concentrated industrial areas have been avoided. Industrialisation came later to Sweden than to some European countries, and so she was able to learn from their mistakes. The Swedes were determined that they would not have dirty, crowded towns. They have long been aware of the need to plan and to keep the towns spacious, light and uncluttered.

The availability of relatively cheap electricity, due to an ample supply of water power, has also been a very important factor in the development of Sweden's industries and in keeping her towns free of dirt and grime. Of course, there are many people who regret the disappearance of vast impressive waterfalls whose torrents are tamed and diverted to produce hydro-electricity, but the benefits of this "white coal", as it is sometimes called, cannot be denied. Sweden is able to produce a quarter of the energy which is used in her homes and industry, from her own hydro-electric plants.

At the present time there is a wide difference of opinion concerning the further development of nuclear power plants in Sweden, which are intended to reduce dependence on imported fuels. A national referendum was held on this matter in 1980. It was decided to keep nuclear power stations but to try to develop alternative sources of energy for the future. This may take as long as twenty-five years.

Although industrialisation did not come very early to Sweden, the rate of development has been far more rapid than in most countries. Conditions just a few decades ago remind one of how they were nearly a hundred years ago elsewhere.

Obviously this has brought many advantages with it, but some problems too. One of these has been the movement of people from the country districts to the towns, especially from the far north. Another has been the growing amount of foreign immigration. People have been attracted by the high standard of living in Sweden, with its social benefits, and the Swedes themselves have preferred to leave the less pleasant, heavy and dirty work to the immigrants.

There are comparatively few parts of Sweden without large forests. The Swedish climate is mainly suitable for softwoods; over a third of the trees are Scots pine and nearly a half are Norwegian spruce. Both of these trees are suitable as sawn wood or for providing pulp. The trunk of the silver birch tree

Timber cutting, the modern way

grows to be very white in the cold, clear Swedish air and this adds to the beauty of the country scene. Unlike the conifers, it loses its leaves in winter. Until a few years ago the silver birch was of little use commercially, and millions of trees were sprayed with chemicals to kill them. This resulted in sad and ugly areas of countryside. Now, however, a method has been developed of using the wood of the silver birch for pulping. It is being used increasingly, so that now one-eighth of the pulp produced is from these trees.

In addition, Swedish matches have been one of the country's best-known export products for many years, and this industry is centred at the town of Jönköping at the southern tip of Lake Vättern.

Although Sweden is situated so far north, the warming effect of the Gulf Stream along the Atlantic coast of the Scandinavian Peninsula allows these vast forests to thrive. Even so, the trees grow twice as fast in the southern provinces as they do in the northern ones. As a tree may take over a hundred years to grow, yet may be felled in a few minutes, great care has to be taken to cultivate new trees all the time. The forests also have to be kept clear, just like weeding a garden. There is always a great dread of forest fires during the often long, dry summer periods. A constant watch is kept and there are repeated warnings by notices, newspapers, radio and television. There are very strict rules about not lighting fires out of doors, away from water, during the months of May to September.

An old photograph
—in the past,
timber was floated
to the saw-mills.
Today, it is sent by
road or rail
instead

For many years the felled timber was hauled over the deep snow in the forests to the frozen rivers; then, when the thaw came, the millions of logs were floated down to the saw-mills. This heavy, dangerous work in the forests and the even more hazardous task of dealing with the log-jams in the rivers, has formed the basis of many exciting stories and has been pictured in a very romantic way. It is no longer possible to see logs being floated down the rivers, as this means of transporting them ceased in 1983. Just as the lumberman's axe has been replaced more and more by power-saws and expensive, efficient machinery which does the work of felling and trimming the trees far more rapidly, so the transportation has been taken over by road and rail, particularly by huge lorries and trailers.

For centuries, the value of the forests lay in their fuel woods, in charcoal for the mining industry, and in the production of tar and lumber for exports. This was followed by a time when the main value was as sawn timber sent to other lands all over the world. The emphasis gradually changed again to the production of wood-pulp and Sweden has become the world's greatest exporter to foreign papermakers. Nowadays paper itself, in a variety of forms including bags, boards and boxes, is as important as pulp.

Although Sweden does not suffer from vast industrial smokey areas, many of these pulping plants produce a most unpleasant smell. Sweden is one of the leading countries in attempts to fight pollution and millions of Swedish kronor are being invested to produce equipment which will limit the impurities discharged into the air and into lakes and rivers.

The Swedish mining industry is mainly concerned with ores. Iron has always played a dominant role in Swedish mining, but at one time copper used to be very important too. The vast copper mine at Falun still attracts thousands of visitors, and there is a very interesting museum there which also offers visits to the underground workings. But the mine no longer produces sufficient ore for Sweden's needs.

Silver was once mined at Sala, but that source is no longer of significance. A small amount of coal is found in Skåne, and this is mainly used in connection with the clay and pottery production at Höganäs. Sweden also has her own sources of uranium, and the extensive wildernesses of the north are being scientifically searched for further supplies of this valuable material.

For several centuries Swedish supplies of wood for charcoal and fires, and water for power, gave the country a leading position in the iron industry. However, when coal and coke fuels were introduced in other countries, Sweden was handicapped by her lack of reserves of this raw material to mass-produce ordinary steel. Nevertheless, the very high quality of Swedish iron, and the steel which is produced from it, has made it greatly valued throughout the world.

The main centres of the iron industry are at Malmberget and Kiruna, which lie north of the Arctic Circle and where mountains consisting almost entirely of iron ore lent themselves originally to easy open-cast mining. It was not even necessary to dig underground to reach the rich deposits. Nowadays, however, deep shafts carrying the most modern mining equipment, yield a plentiful supply.

Kiruna is one of the largest towns in the world—not in size of population, as that is less than 30,000 people, but in its huge

Kiruna, with the iron ore mines in the background

area—13,181 square kilometres (over 5,000 square miles). The borders include vast unpopulated areas and several mountains, amongst them being Kebnekaise, which has a peak at 2,117 metres (about 7,000 feet) and is Sweden's highest. And there are many glaciers in this region.

43

To transport the vast quantities of ore from the far north, the mining districts were connected by rail to Luleå, a large port on the Baltic coast. In spite of the efforts of ice-breakers, however, it was not possible to keep these waters free of ice in the severe winter months, and so, at the end of the nineteenth century a railway line was built right over the top of the mountains to the Norwegian port of Narvik. This remarkable feat of engineering gave access to an ice-free port and greatly helped to increase Sweden's export trade. This rail journey is most impressive and beautiful, but the frequent long trains with numerous trucks of iron-ore serve as a reminder of the original reason for the existence of this route.

Special steels, such as alloy and high carbon steels, make up about a third of Sweden's total steel production. One very important product is roller- and ball-bearings, and the Swedish SKF ball-bearings are known throughout the world. They literally keep the wheels of industry turning. Sandvik steel is another well-known name. Many of the saws used throughout the world come from the Swedish town of Sandviken, which lies about three hours' drive north of Stockholm, in the province of Gästrikland. It was here, in 1858, that the world's first steel was made on an industrial scale by a new method, called the Bessemer process.

Linked to iron and steel production is the important shipbuilding industry. The Swedish merchant navy is expanding more rapidly than ever before and new ships are being built on a large scale. Since the beginning of the 1960s the fleet has been almost renewed and more and more supertankers are being built. The ice-breaking fleet has been increased so that it is now possible to keep most of the northern ports open throughout the winter, at least when conditions are not excessively severe.

Sweden builds ships for other countries too, and is among the world's leading shipbuilding nations. Her shipyards are situated on the west coast, from Göteborg (Gothenburg) to Malmö, in the south. They are mainly owned by the shipping companies and co-operation between them plays an important part in the success of this industry.

Sweden is the most motorized country in Europe. In 1981 there were 2·9 million passenger cars in this land with only about eight million inhabitants, i.e. approximately one car for every three people.

Sweden has two large-scale car manufacturing companies: Volvo and Saab-Scania. Volvo is the largest industrial company in Sweden. Saab manufactures aircraft as well as cars.

A shipyard at Göteborg

The cars which these companies produce are designed to stand up to rugged winter conditions and to the rough roads in some of the many remote areas. Great attention is, of course, paid to safety in the design and construction of these Swedish vehicles. There has been a growing appreciation of these qualities in Swedish cars in other countries, and now almost three out of every four cars produced are exported.

Although industries connected with the natural supplies of timber and iron ore have long been one of the main sources of Sweden's national wealth, during the years since the Second World War, Sweden's chemical industry has outstripped them in rate of growth. This has been particularly rapid for organic chemicals, plastics, pharmaceuticals and, more recently, in the petro-chemical industry. But these industries connected with chemicals are not all new. The inventor Alfred Nobel founded his munitions works which eventually developed into a world-wide enterprise as long ago as 1864. In his will, Nobel left money to be used for the famous prizes which are given annually for outstanding contributions in the fields of physics, chemistry, physiology and medicine, literature and peace.

Less than one-tenth of the total area of Sweden is arable land, suitable for cultivation. Although the climatic conditions vary a great deal between the north and south, Sweden really enjoys a climate which is far warmer and more suitable for agriculture than other non-Scandinavian countries in the same northerly latitudes.

Farmers in the southern coastal areas grow a wide range of crops. The yield of wheat is good and much sugar beet is grown. The southernmost province of Skåne (Scania) is sometimes referred to as the Granary of Sweden. However, a lot of grain for flour and for animal feeding is also grown on the flat plains in central Sweden. Farther north, the proportion of crops grown as fodder is higher.

About three-quarters of the Swedish harvest provides fodder for livestock. This is important, as about eighty per cent of the farmers' income is from animal production. Cattle are the most usual type of livestock. The herds are usually small, because the animals cannot graze out-of-doors in the long winter months, but must be kept warm under cover. The number of dairy cows has decreased sharply in recent years but, on the other hand, the production of beef calves has increased. Pig-breeding is also widespread. In general, the number of small herds is declining. This is typical of all Swedish agriculture where the tendency is to replace small farms by larger units.

Poultry farming used to be a mere side-line until quite recent years, but now it is growing into an independent occupation. Egg production is being taken over more and more by large, specialized chicken farms. Broilers are raised in large efficient units.

Sheep-farming has started to become a more significant alternative to beef stock in Sweden in recent years. There are the white sheep mainly for slaughter and the grey sheep which provide curly fleece as well as meat. The island of Gotland, in the Baltic, is particularly well-known as a sheep-rearing area.

Swedish economy has changed tremendously in the past one hundred years. As recently as 1880, agriculture was still Sweden's principal industry, employing about three-quarters of the population. Then came the rapid growth of towns and cities, and the decline of the agricultural population. In 1980 only three per cent of the people were working in agriculture.

Swedish farms are growing in size but becoming fewer in number. The farming is still being largely carried on by family enterprise and the land is generally worked by the people who own it. However, the average age of farmers is rising. Most smaller farms have nobody who can take over after the present farmer.

The proportion of co-operative organisations, which market and process the agricultural produce is higher in Sweden than in most other countries. Thus, dairy products are refined completely within the farmers' co-operative organizations. About eighty-five per cent of all meat production comes from co-operative slaughterhouses.

Fishing is nowadays not such an important industry in Sweden as it was, nor as it still is in Denmark and Norway. Some hundreds of years ago the Baltic herring were a main Swedish export, but these fish migrated to the North Sea and Norway's Atlantic coast. Now the main fishing area in Sweden is in Bohuslän, north of Göteborg (Gothenburg). The herring, cod, mackerel and shellfish which are still caught, form an important part of Sweden's food production, but fewer young men now choose the hard, often dangerous, life of a fisherman. In addition, the recent discussions and decisions about extending the fishing limits of many nations have threatened to seriously affect the opportunities for Swedish west-coast fishermen.

Sweden is a very active trading nation, with trading partners in all parts of the world, but roughly three-quarters of Swedish foreign trade is with western Europe. The goods produced by the various industries must be delivered to the people who are going to use them, either in other parts of Sweden, or abroad. Similarly, the goods brought from abroad must be delivered to all parts of Sweden. But transportation not only means the movement of goods from place to place, people have to be transported as well. There has been an ever-growing tendency to concentrate on rail transport for long distances in the length of Sweden and to use motor transport for journeys across the width of the land.

Trains are used for really long-distance haulage on a number of main lines, mostly in the north-to-south direction. In relation to its size of population, Sweden has the largest railway network in Europe with 12,000 kilometres (7,500 miles) of track. The railways are almost entirely served by modern electric and diesel trains.

Road-building in Sweden is made difficult by the often severe winter conditions. The depth to which frost penetrates the ground causes considerable damage to the road surface. In all, the road network consists of about 330,000 kilometres (over 200,000 miles). Of course, these figures include the very isolated roads which carry comparatively little traffic. The main routes are of a high standard, and long distance motoring in Sweden is quite pleasant, at least, in the summer months. However, there are no "cat's eyes" to help indicate the centre and sides of the road. They would not survive the action of the winter frost, and would soon become covered by snow or torn up by the snow ploughs. In such wintry conditions it is difficult to judge just where the road ends and the ditch begins. To help with this problem, canes—or even just slender branches—carrying reflectors are staked along the sides of the roads in autumn. These protrude above the snow and mark the edge of the road-surface.

Although Sweden has more cars per head of population than any other European country, the size of the country absorbs them easily, and it is not difficult to cover long distances travelling nearly all the time at the maximum permitted speed. The large towns and cities have their parking problems and congested traffic, but the cars, large lorries and trailers flow out easily on wide roads, in spite of the fact that Sweden has few motorways.

Although the winter conditions present difficulties, these problems are expected and the many snow-ploughs are in action almost as soon as the first flakes fall. Motorists fit specially studded tyres to their cars in the winter months. Snow clearing is, however, very expensive for Sweden's economy, and so is the damage done to the modern road surfaces by the snow-ploughs and metal-studded tyres.

As rail fares have increased, there has been a rapid growth in the use of long-distance buses in Sweden in recent years. The State Railways also operate an express bus service between a number of cities. The Post Office runs a fleet of buses for deliveries of letters and packages to the more remote areas, and these bright yellow vehicles also carry a small number of passengers at a not too expensive fare.

Air travel within Sweden has increased during the past decade, but it is still not as popularly used as in some other lands. International flights mainly use the airports of Malmö, Göteborg (Gothenburg) and Stockholm. Arlanda is the airport for international flights to the capital, and it must strike most visitors as being very modern. It has recently been extended to cope with "jumbo" jets and the ever-increasing number of charter flights which carry the Swedes to more southerly latitudes for a week or more of much needed sunshine during the long winter months.

An SAS plane at Stockholm's Arlanda airport (note the snow on the ground)

Swedish air transport is best known internationally through SAS, the Scandinavian Airline System. SAS is owned jointly by Danish, Norwegian and Swedish companies, and each is owned half by the State and half by private interests. SAS is a good example of practical co-operation between neighbouring countries, as none of these three small nations could have established itself in international air traffic as SAS has done. In 1984 SAS was voted "Airline of the Year".

Domestic shipping in Sweden has tended to be limited to a few special types of cargo such as stone, pyrites and petroleum. There are about two hundred ports along the 2,500 kilometres (just over 1,500 miles) of sea and lake shores. There are also interior waterways on the many lakes, and some canals. The name Göta Canal is quite often used to refer to the full extent of the waterway between Göteborg (Gothenburg) and Stockholm, but actually it is the stretch which connects the lakes Vänern and Vättern. Although its commercial value dwindled many years ago, it still provides a very popular tourist attraction.

During the winter, ice-breakers are required to keep open the Baltic Sea ports, especially those in the North. One operates on Lake Vänern, so that its harbours can operate the whole year round. In other areas, however, the frozen lakes provide an opportunity for cars, lorries and sometimes even buses to save considerable distances on their journeys, by following marked routes over the ice, though obviously this can only be done when conditions are safe.

Cities and Towns

As many Swedes have moved into the towns from the country, this has meant an internal migration of the population towards the southern third of Sweden where the three largest cities are situated. They are: Stockholm, the capital and second largest port, with a population of about 1,400,000; then comes Göteborg (Gothenburg), the largest port, with nearly 700,000 people; whilst Malmö, in the most southerly province of Skåne (Scania), is both the third largest city and the third largest port, with nearly half a million inhabitants. These three cities alone contain not far short of one-third of the entire population, which is just over eight million.

STOCKHOLM

The beautiful setting of Stockholm makes it one of the most attractive capitals in Europe. It has grown up around a small island in Lake Mälaren, where it was founded seven hundred years ago. From ground level it is difficult to visualise the size of Lake Mälaren and to realise that it is the third largest lake in the country. But viewed from the air the numerous branches and inlets of the lake are more easily seen as belonging to one vast sheet of water. From the aeroplane, flying north over Stockholm to land at Arlanda, it is easy to see how the capital has been given the name of "Venice of the North". Like that famous Italian city, Stockholm is divided by numerous waterways which beautify the city.

At ground level it is, perhaps, easier to see how Stockholm also came to be called "The City between the Bridges". From the oldest part of the original city, known as Gamla Stan (Old Town), the modern capital has spread out to the north, west and south to about a dozen or so islands. These are all linked by many bridges. The narrow cobblestone alleys in the Old Town, in which one can literally touch houses on opposite sides of the "street" at the same time, contrast strikingly with the modern bridges. These magnificent examples of engineering and construction also have their own form of beauty. A popular trip for visitors to Stockholm is to go by boat under many of the city's bridges. It is a very good way of seeing this attractive capital.

As Stockholm has spread, many suburbs have grown. These

A view of Stockholm from the tower of the City Hall

small towns contain many blocks of apartments and the buildings tend to be functional rather than beautiful. Much time and money goes into the planning of these suburbs, and the standard of the facilities provided is very high. Pedestrian shopping centres, free of traffic, and numerous play-parks for children are always included. Modern sculpture and fountains abound. Every effort is made to preserve trees around the sites, but obviously such homes differ greatly from smaller, individual houses and gardens. By living in these blocks of apartments, people are spared many of the inconveniences associated with the winter, such as clearing away the snow from paths and driveways. The multi-storey buildings provide communal facilities in the extensive basement areas. There are laundry-rooms with large washing-machines, driers and carpet cleaners, as well as big areas for storage of cycles and skis. Many include a cherished heated garage under ground. For cars parked outside these apartments during the winter, there are usually electric heaters into which the car may be plugged.

Stockholm could not spread to the east for there lies the Baltic Sea. However, the entrance to the capital city and important port is dotted with thousands of small islands which make up the Stockholm Archipelago. Such clusters of islands are also called skerries. They provide a wonderful playground for the Stockholmers. There is a regular fleet of small, picturesque old steamers which link Stockholm with the islands and there is plenty of room in the extensive archipelago for numerous sailing vessels and motor boats of all sorts, colours and sizes. On the islands there are thousands of cabins and cottages where many families live for the whole of the summer.

It is quite common for people in Sweden to have a second, often quite simple, home, especially if they live in an apartment building. They probably do not miss having a plot of ground, or garden, of their own, during the winter months. But in the summer they love to spend as much time as possible close to nature. Now, however, some people prefer to live in an individual house with its own little plot of land, and so Stockholm continues to expand.

The capital is the only Swedish town with an underground train service. It is not easy to tunnel in this city of rock and water, and much of the outer part of the network is above ground. The area which is served is being steadily extended, so that more and more modern stations are made available from which the thousands of commuters may be transported daily to the central parts of the city, and thus reduce the pressure on road traffic and the almost inevitable bottlenecks formed by the many bridges.

Like all capital cities, Stockholm has many attractions for the myriads of visitors. Amongst the most popular is Skansen. Although it is also a zoo, its main charm is as an open-air museum. The Swedes are very conscious of the need to preserve a record of their past. Here, at Skansen, is a collection which has been made from a wide area. It is not only the foreign visitors, but the Swedes themselves, who are interested to walk around old churches, houses, shops, mills, workshops

56

A view of Stockholm, "The City between the Bridges"

and farm buildings from years gone by, and to see the furniture and equipment which they contain.

A vivid contrast to Skansen is provided by a visit to nearby Kaknästornet, a modern television tower and the tallest building in the Nordic countries. From the restaurant, or viewing platform, near the top, there is a magnificent view over the city. Most days are clear and one can see right across to the western outskirts of the city. To the east there is a fine view of the archipelago and the busy shipping lanes. The armada of thousands of vessels of all sizes leaving Stockholm on a Friday evening, or returning again late on Sunday, is a most remarkable sight.

57

The Stadshuset (City Hall)

Dominating the city, on the shore of the lake, is the stately building of Stadshuset, the City Hall, which was completed in 1923. The three golden crowns which glisten at the very top of the impressive red brick tower are a landmark from all directions.

Across the waters can be seen the old Houses of Parliament. During the 1970s, the offices of government were housed in a functional glass-faced building close to the five skyscrapers which tower over the city centre. But now Parliament meets once again in the original Riksdag building, and the modern structure has become an important international conference centre.

Next to the old Houses of Parliament stands the large square building of the Royal Palace. Almost on its front doorstep is the quayside from which regular ferry-boats ply to Finland and the Finnish Baltic island of Åland. Close by is Slussen, where a lock links Lake Mälaren with the sea. This is also the site of Stockholm's most impressive clover-leaf road system, where a busy stream of traffic negotiates the routes connecting the various islands which form this old part of the city. Near by, too, is Strömmen, another link with the open sea. And here may be seen the picturesque small fishing-boats with their circular fishing nets.

Another very interesting item on the list of visits to be made in Stockholm, is the warship *Wasa* and the museum connected with her. She sank at the very commencement of her maiden voyage in 1628. Some of her valuable cannon were salvaged soon afterwards by divers using primitive diving-bells. But the vessel, and all that she contained, remained on the bottom of the waters not far from the very centre of Stockholm, until she was re-discovered in 1956. The lifting of the shipwreck was a remarkable achievement, and the care with which the water-logged vessel has been protected and preserved has provided expert and laymen visitors alike with a unique opportunity to see just how a seventeenth-century warship was equipped, and

The warship *Wasa* in dry dock

what everyday articles were in use. The vessel has been gradually restored and rebuilt, where necessary, and the aim is to present her to the public in her full, original and colourful glory. A new Wasa Museum is expected to be completed in about 1990.

The eyes of visitors to Stockholm are caught by the sight of another, more graceful, old sailing ship. This is the *af Chapman* as she lies permanently at anchor on the stretch of water opposite the Royal Palace. Nowadays she is pressed into service as a youth hostel, busily providing cheap accommodation for the night to the thousands upon thousands of young visitors who come every year to this beautiful capital.

GÖTEBORG (GOTHENBURG)

Stockholm's only real rival, as a city of importance, is Göteborg. This city, which is sometimes called Gothenburg, is 492 kilometres (about 300 miles) away on the west coast. It is nothing like as old as the capital, having been founded in the seventeenth century. It grew up around the site of some previous settlements at this obvious position for defending the entrance to the Göta River. The name Göteborg means, in fact "The Göta Fortress".

From its earliest days, Göteborg has been a busy trading centre, and many of the influential inhabitants there were foreigners. Dutch, German, English and Scottish merchants, in particular, played an important role in the development of the city.

Göteborg, Sweden's largest port and her second city

The imposing canal still to be seen in the middle of Göteborg is a reminder of the Dutch who built it and planned the straight wide streets of the city. There were, originally, more of these canals, but they have since been filled in to provide other highways.

Göteborg's importance is nearly all connected with the sea. It is Sweden's largest port, the home of the very important shipbuilding industry, and also the largest fishing port.

Many other industries are situated there too. The country's biggest factory producing motor vehicles for the Volvo company is in Göteborg, and so is the main factory making SKF ball- and roller-bearings.

Yet, in spite of these industries, it is not necessary to travel far from the centre of Göteborg to reach a most attractive holiday area, where thousands of visitors enjoy sailing, swimming and sunbathing amongst the shimmering waters and rocky islets of the archipelago. Dotted along the coast are hundreds of delightful, old red-painted fisher-cottages, now mostly in use as summer dwellings.

Unspoiled beaches like this one are a feature of Sweden's coasts, particularly on the islands not far from Göteborg.

Malmö's Town Hall, built in 1546, restored in 1812 and again in 1864

MALMÖ

Malmö is the most important city in the part of Sweden which has much of its past linked with Denmark. It is the leading trading and industrial centre of Skåne. Malmö was founded by the Danes in the beginning of the twelfth century. At this

63

point, only the narrow straits of Öresund separate the Swedish coast from the Danish capital of Copenhagen. Serious proposals have been made to build a bridge between the two countries in this region. This would relieve the pressure on the very busy ferry services across this stretch of water with its heavy sea traffic. Such a bridge would be even longer than the present longest in Europe, which was opened in 1972 to link the mainland of Sweden to the Baltic island of Öland nearly $4\frac{1}{2}$ miles (seven kilometres) away.

Apart from these three large cities, there are many other towns in Sweden which have special attractions for visitors. One of these is Visby, the main town on the island of Gotland, in the Baltic Sea. This is one of Sweden's old cities. More than six hundred years ago it was one of the most active Baltic ports.

The traders realised that their riches were attractive to raiders and invading armies, and so a great protective wall was built around the city. However, it did not keep out the Danes who overran Visby in 1361. Since then the city has never regained its importance. Visby is still "invaded" every summer, by thousands of tourists and holiday-makers who cross from the mainland to enjoy the charms of this "City of Ruins and Roses".

Another city with a wealth of historical interest, is Uppsala. It lies to the north of Stockholm, just an hour's journey along the motorway. This is the largest city in the province of Uppland with a population around 150,000.

It was in this region that many of the early settlements were established; and the tribes of Swedes had a capital there long before Stockholm was founded. There was an important temple at what is now called Gamla Uppsala (Old Uppsala) and the burial mounds there attract numerous visitors. It was these tumuli, or barrows, that were the burial places of the Viking leaders.

Since Christianity came to Sweden, the Church of Sweden has been centred on Uppsala. It is here that the archbishop has his cathedral. Many of the early Swedish kings were buried at Uppsala cathedral.

Not far from the cathedral is Sweden's oldest university. The several thousands of students in Uppsala have earned for this picturesque town the name of "The City of Eternal Youth".

Uppsala Cathedral, which dates back to the thirteenth century and is the largest church in Scandinavia

**Vasa Castle
(in the foreground
is the bell tower)**

On the hill, overlooking the surrounding plains, is a huge, solid castle with vast circular towers. It is Vasa Castle, built in the days of Gustav Vasa. This building, together with the twin cathedral spires, dominates the Uppsala skyline. Although there is now a considerable amount of industry in Uppsala, it is mostly situated around the outskirts of the city.

Not far from Uppsala is the tiny town of Sigtuna with its one narrow main street with very old shops, many of which still have their trade signs hanging outside, just as attractively as they did well over a hundred years ago. This place, too, was once of very great importance as a leading community, or "capital", for the early inhabitants. It was founded in the eleventh century. The old town hall, built in 1744, and one of the smallest in the world, still stands. But only the ruins of four ancient churches, and a few rune stones, remind us of past glories. Possibly only Sigtuna School has any claim to present-day fame. It is one of the very few remaining private schools in Sweden, and was attended by the present king of Sweden when he was a young student.

It is not only in the big cities that the visitor to Sweden finds interest and pleasure, but also in the many small towns and villages such as this.

The picturesque town of Sigtuna

Education and Social Welfare

If fine buildings and facilities help to make a good educational system, then the Swedes should certainly have an excellent one. During the last two decades millions of kronor, raised by taxes, have been spent on completely reshaping the Swedish schools and most of what is taught in them. The many small village schools have been replaced by centralised modern buildings and curriculum reforms have brought about a wide choice of subjects leading to courses which are appropriate to all levels of ability. There are full opportunities for everyone. "Equality" has been a slogan of the governing politicians in Sweden for many years, and it underlines the whole of the Swedish school system.

An outstanding feature of the Swedish school system is the standardisation. The subjects that will be taught at each age-level, the standard that will be reached in those subjects, and how many lessons per week, are the same in all the compulsory comprehensive schools throughout the land. At the same time, the syllabuses are not rigid but provide broad general frameworks. Textbooks that are used must normally be selected from those approved by the education authorities.

Education is compulsory for all children between the ages of seven and sixteen.

Normally, Swedish schools start at eight o'clock in the morning and the length of the school day may vary for individual age-groups. There is usually a break of ten minutes between lessons and often the children have a period during which they are allowed to leave the school grounds. All comprehensive schools are for boys and girls together. There is no school uniform and jeans are worn by most children, girls and boys alike. Schoolchildren usually wear wooden clogs with leather tops. This type of footwear is quite common for older people as well; when one is used to clogs, they are comfortable to wear even when running, jumping, climbing and cycling.

The schools are well equipped and all books and materials are provided without charge. There is also free dental care for schoolchildren. Free lunches are provided for all pupils every day, and there is no fare for transportation to school by bus, or taxi, when the authorities consider that such means of travel are necessary.

The school year is divided into two terms. From the end of August there is a long term until the two weeks' holiday for Christmas, apart from a short mid-term break. The second term has a week's holiday at the end of February, or the beginning of March, for winter sports. The actual date is staggered throughout the country to enable the thousands of children to participate in organised parties or in individual holidays, when many get away to the mountains for ski-ing. This is a much longed-for break in the otherwise rather dreary winter period with its short hours of daylight. The Easter holiday is a short one of little more than a week, but then spring is on the way, and the long summer holiday, which usually lasts nearly three months begins very early in June.

Although compulsory primary schooling ends at the age of sixteen, about ninety per cent of the young people continue their schooling in the "gymnasium" or secondary school, for a further period of two to four years. In some cases the distances to these gymnasium schools are too great to allow daily travelling, so that living accommodation near the school has to be found. There are generous grants made to all young people to encourage them to continue their education. There is a wide range of courses available to them, either leading to still further studies at colleges or universities, or in training for business, industry or trade.

The oldest universities were founded at Uppsala (in 1477), and Lund (in 1666). Those at Göteborg (Gothenburg) and Stockholm are more modern but are well established. More recent still is the university of Umeå, in Norrland, and the university colleges of Karlstad, Linköping, Örebro and Växjö. There is strong competition for entrance into some of the of the university courses and these newer universities and colleges have been opened to meet the demand for places. Students who attend colleges and universities receive a basic grant; in addition they usually take an interest-free loan, which has to be repaid within a period of fifteen years.

Every effort is made to see that the well-equipped Swedish school buildings are put to good use. The classrooms and sporting facilities, inside and outside the building, are available to the whole community. For example, the swimming-pool is used by the pupils during the school day, and by the general public afterwards. Adult education is also very widespread in Sweden, and the buildings are put to good use in that way also.

As well as attendance by adults at the normal local school, there is also a specifically Scandinavian form of further education for those who did not continue their schooling beyond the compulsory period. This is the Folk High School, a type of boarding-school, which offers a wide variety of 22– to 34–week courses during the winter months. Many of these schools offer other shorter, specific courses. There is very much less standardisation in the Folk High Schools. In all, about one adult in every three, between the ages of twenty and sixty-five, takes part in some form of adult education.

All of this has to be paid for, of course, although it is called "free". Swedish taxes are high compared with most countries. In addition to income tax there is a communal tax. Both the income and communal taxes are "pay-as-you-earn" schemes. In addition to these different taxes there is also a value-added tax.

Nearly all people in all countries grumble about the taxes they have to pay. But it must be remembered that much of the revenues the taxes yield are returned to the citizens as payments of some kind or other, at some future date, or as public services. Swedish taxes are relatively high, but the social services are extensive.

Sweden's social welfare programme aims to protect the individual against any threat to his livelihood. There is a compulsory general insurance coverage for illness, childbirth, disablement, old age and loss of the family bread-winner.

Swedish hospitals have long enjoyed a good international reputation for their high standards of equipment and medical care. The medical service in an open ward is quite free of charge. There is, however, growing concern over the waiting time for entry into hospital for non-emergency cases.

At the beginning of 1974 a national insurance scheme came into effect, so that half of the cost of dental treatment is re-funded.

Sweden has the world's lowest infant death rate and lowest rate of childbirth mortality. At the other end of the age scale, the average length of life is amongst the longest in the world.

Sweden has a fast-increasing number of elderly people and by 1983 nearly seventeen per cent of the population (about one and a half million people) had reached retirement age. These elderly citizens receive a retirement pension and there are also good pension schemes to help widows and orphans.

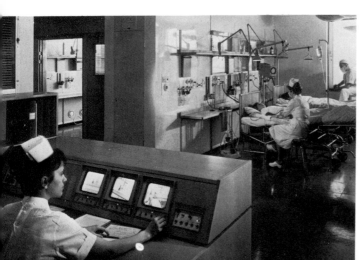

Two patients being treated in one of Sweden's many modern hospitals

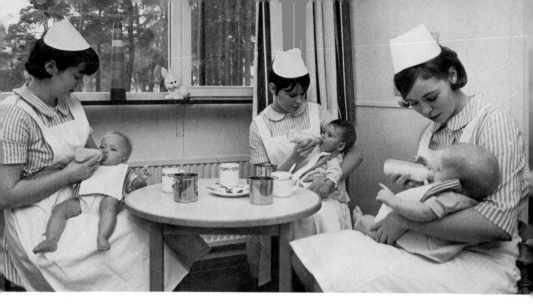

Three of Sweden's youngest citizens. Child care is given high priority in the state's medical and social services

Like many other countries, Sweden has difficulty in providing employment for all her workers, and so financial help has to be given to the unemployed. In this field, and that of disability payments, Sweden is recognised as being one of the countries which has set an example to others. These measures, and other forms of social aid in cases of special need, together with housing subsidies, mean that real poverty and slums are almost a thing of the past in Sweden.

Unfortunately, even these well-meaning reforms have not solved all the social problems. The amount of drunkenness in Sweden is still a cause of great concern.

Sports and Pastimes

The Swedes are a very active people. They love sport. Generally they choose individual sports like sailing, ski-ing, fishing and hiking, rather than more formal team games. Nevertheless, there are, of course, many Swedes who enjoy team games and sports which feature a ball.

Many internationally known sports are played in Sweden, but cricket, baseball, grass-court tennis, outdoor bowling, land hockey (so-called to distinguish it from ice-hockey), lacrosse, netball and rounders are almost unknown. Rugby football is also very much a minority sport.

On the other hand, Swedes participate in the sports made possible by the thousands of lakes and the cold winters in their

Ice yachting on one of Sweden's many lakes

A fishing competition. Competitors fish through holes in the ice

country. All young children are taught to swim by instructors at school, if they cannot do so already. A Swedish non-swimmer is quite a rarity. Water ski-ing is becoming a very popular, although expensive, pastime. The winter ice brings out people of all ages to enjoy all kinds of activities. Figure skating and long-distance skating both have their attraction. Some skaters add to their speed, and test their skill, by carrying a sail. Others sit in an ice-yacht and skim across the frozen lake.

The Swedes are well-known for their ability as motor-racing drivers, rally drivers, motor-cyclists, speedway and moto-cross drivers. In the winter, they even have car and motor-cycle races on ice, to add an extra thrill. Cycling has become less common in the busy town traffic during recent decades, but cycles still appear as a form of pleasurable exercise. There are repeated campaigns to encourage people to cycle, in order to save fuel and reduce traffic congestion and also for health reasons.

The Swedes are extremely keen on physical fitness and many homes have a special fixed cycle in the cellar to provide an opportunity for pedalling away indoors when weather conditions outside are too bad. It is quite common to see Swedes of both sexes, and a variety of ages and shapes, dressed

75

in track suits and jogging around the streets or nearby country-side. For many of the youngsters, though, it is the motorised cycle, or moped, which provides their transport in a less energetic and more noisy way. Mopeds may be used on public roads by drivers who have reached the age of fifteen. So, when the ice on the lakes is thick enough, mopeds and even cars, join the skaters. They must all keep an eye open for the fisherman, probably crouched on a portable stool, waiting patiently for a bite at the end of the line which he has lowered through the hole he has drilled in the ice. The small "trees" seen "growing" out of the frozen lake are in reality the branches subsequently left by the fishermen to warn the unwary of the danger of the holes.

The Swedes are very keen fishermen and there are wonderful opportunities for enjoying this sport throughout the country. Although a fishing licence is required in some areas, there are still plenty of rivers and lakes without such restrictions. Many visitors to Sweden go there just for the fishing.

The mountains attract thousands of holiday-makers every year, and mountain walking is very popular amongst the Swedes themselves. The Swedish Tourist Association provides help with simple but adequate accommodation, with safety controls and by marking tracks. However, everything is done to leave the wild areas as unspoiled as possible. A more formal way of enjoying the countryside is the popular sport of orient-eering.

Ski-ing is enjoyed by most Swedes, and they feel that they

have been deprived if they do not get a "real" winter, with plenty of snow. Cross-country ski-ing has become rather less popular amongst the younger generation, but down-hill and slalom ski-ing has gained in popularity. Many towns still, however, provide an illuminated ski-track through a nearby forest for the many thousands of enthusiasts who still enjoy cross-country ski-ing. Some Swedes now travel abroad to ski on the steeper mountain slopes of other countries where the hours of winter daylight are longer. There are, of course, many fine ski resorts in the mountainous districts of Sweden but, for a Swede living in the southern part of his long country, these may be almost as far away and as expensive as those abroad. In some places there are ski-jumps, but these are less common in Sweden than in neighbouring Norway.

Ice-hockey is the favourite pastime of many Swedish boys. During the winter months the school playground is flooded and the boys spend most of their spare time with a puck and stick, even if they do not always have their skates on. Swedish school playgrounds are not locked and fenced off, so that playing areas are available out of school hours. There are also many well-lit open-air rinks on which to play. Most of the nationally known teams play their matches on artificially frozen ice in indoor rinks where they are keenly supported.

A typically Swedish sport is bandy, which is similar to ice-hockey, but is played with a ball instead of the flat, circular puck. This game is played on a rink with the same dimensions as a soccer field. Another uniquely Swedish sport is varpa, which is similar to both discus-throwing and horse-shoe pitching. This ancient sport comes from Gotland.

Soccer is the Swedish national sport in the summer-time, and it is usually played during the times of the year which come before and after the ice-hockey season. Most games are played on non-grass surfaces, although many of the major teams play on turfed pitches. Recent experiments with artificial, plastic-type "grass" promise improvements. Soccer has gained considerable following in the last twenty years and there is rapidly growing interest in girls' soccer.

Gymnastics, athletics, table-tennis, volley-ball and hand-ball are popular, and there has been increased interest recently in ten-pin bowling, basket-ball, badminton and squash. Tennis has long had fair support, during the summer months. The international successes of Björn Borg, followed by Mats Wilander, at this sport have caught the imagination of other youngsters and the following has grown remarkably. There is a great demand for more indoor facilities, and some of this is being met by huge, inflatable tennis halls.

The winter climate is not kind to golf enthusiasts, but a series of mild winters in recent years has helped to increase the number of players who enjoy this sport.

Sport is obviously not the only form of recreation in which the Swedes indulge. They have the same interests and opportunities as are found in other countries with a similar background. There are plenty of chances to enjoy music of all

78

kinds, whether at live performances or through radio and television.

Sweden has two television channels and both are non-commercial. Being a small nation, Sweden has to buy many of her television programmes from other countries and this involves the frequent need for sub-titles. Some of the best Swedish artists, performers and entertainers leave their small home-country, with its minority language, to seek larger audiences and wider opportunities abroad.

Language differences also have their effect on books. The limited number of editions in the Swedish language means that the prices of books are high. However, the Swedes have long been aware that to get the best out of life, they must have a good command of other languages. English is the first foreign language taught in schools, and most Swedes are well able to read, understand and converse in it. Many can do equally well in one or more other foreign language as well.

Theatres are well supported in Sweden, and travelling companies are subsidised in order to bring this form of culture to the more remote areas. Cinemas, too, have survived the difficult times which they faced after the introduction of television. Their performances are non-continuous, and normally are confined to the evening. Smoking is not permitted in Swedish theatres or cinemas.

The Swedes have also invested a lot of money in the provision of youth clubs in order to provide recreational facilities for young people.

Swedish Design

The high standard and distinctive quality of Swedish design enjoys a world-wide reputation. It is its simplicity and clarity of form which is most striking. It is noticeable in the display windows of shops that the quality of the goods they sell is generally good and that there are few cheap, shoddy things. This does not only apply to the large city stores. The Swedish consumer obviously expects value for his money and good taste in objects about him. It is in the design and quality of material things that the Swedish high standard of living is reflected. It is in industrial arts, handicrafts and architecture that the term "Swedish Modern" has arisen, and it is in these fields that a remarkable development has taken place in this century.

Some examples of Swedish design and craftsmanship – simple but beautiful

Both the wooden cross and the wooden birds in this picture are hand-carved

The success of Swedish design is partly based upon a conscious attempt to preserve and revive the traditions of the eighteenth century. The industrial revolution of the nineteenth century nearly succeeded in wiping out the creative artists with their traditional Swedish handicrafts.

Textile art is, perhaps, the best example of a home-craft which has combined the need of a rural population to create useful objects with their desire to achieve a pleasing appearance. Old techniques and ancient weaving designs have been copied and later adapted by present-day artists. A weaving loom is not an uncommon object in the spare room, or cellar, of a Swedish home. Weaving is popular amongst young and old alike; in schools and in pensioners' homes.

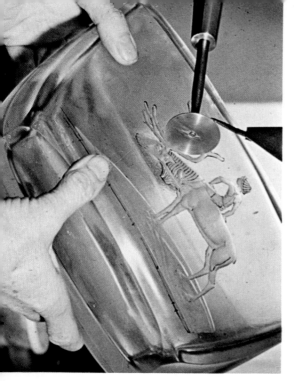

Engraving a piece of Orrefors glass. Swedish glass is world famous for its quality, design and engraving

Most Swedes appreciate their country's old crafts and are keen to preserve them. In many towns you will see a shop bearing the name *Hemslöjd*, where genuine handicrafts are on sale. The purchase of rural antiques is very popular too. Carved furniture, wooden implements and utensils are eagerly sought, and so are tools and kitchenware made from wrought iron and copper.

Swedish design is very well-known in glassware. Crystal from the most famous glassworks of Orrefors, Kosta and Boda is always a popular souvenir for visitors from all parts of the world. The glass industry is concentrated in a small area of the province of Småland, where there happened to be good supplies of the kind of sand which is needed in the glass-making process. Life was hard in Sweden at the end of the nineteenth century and a large proportion of the Swedes who emigrated came from this southern province. But the people from Småland are well-known and respected for their ingenuity and ability to work hard. Perhaps it was this determination to find an alternative form of livelihood to the vain struggle with their surrounding land that helped to develop the skilled craft of glass-making in Småland. As well as the high quality of the glass and the appeal of the attractive shapes, it is the beautiful engraving which has contributed to the success of the Swedish glass industry.

In articles of pottery and stainless steel, the combination of design and quality often makes them easily recognizable as being of Swedish origin. Kitchen- and table-ware from Sweden are particularly successful and popular.

Swedish furniture also enjoys a good international reputation and is greatly in demand, as much for its modern design as for its functional efficiency.

Sometimes characteristically Nordic design appears in Swedish architecture, though this is more likely to happen in expensive office buildings (partly intended to create an air of wealth and modernity) or in public buildings and monuments. Normal everyday building is not particularly attractive on the outside. It is more likely to be rather starkly designed to fulfil its purpose. But inside homes and offices the emphasis is placed on quality and good design.

The Lapps

The Lapps have lived in Sweden for thousands of years. Many clues point to the fact that they migrated from eastern lands at various times, in different groups, in the years before Christianity. Their language is quite unlike Swedish; the fact that it is similar to Finnish fits in with the theory that the original tribes came via southern Finland and the shores of the Arctic Sea. Their appearance, too, has eastern characteristics. The Lapps are short and generally much darker than the Swedes. Their colouring, their high cheek bones and somewhat slanting eyes all give them an oriental look. Their bodies are sturdy and wiry.

The Lapps, also known as Samer, are a proud people with a quiet air of dignity. They settled in northernmost Sweden so long ago that their claim to the territories there can be regarded as an ancient right, and that is generally respected by Swedish law.

The area of Lapp settlement stretches over the entire arctic region and extends through Russia and Finland as well as on both sides of the Norwegian-Swedish border and down to the northern part of the province of Dalarna (Dalecarlia).

Originally the Lapps were hunters and fishermen. The capturing, and eventual taming, of wild reindeer became a feature of their way of life over a thousand years. They lived as nomads, following their herds up to the pastures in the mountains in the spring and down to the wooded lowlands in the autumn. It

Nomadic Lapps and their reindeer

is too cold and bleak for plants to grow on the high hills and mountain slopes north of the Arctic Circle. There is not enough food to support sheep or goats, but reindeer are able to find grazing in the form of lichen and moss.

The nomadic Lapps were almost completely dependent on the reindeer for food—in the form of meat and milk; for clothing and tents—from the skins; and for transport—by using

85

the larger reindeer as draught animals. Still today the Lapps are also very skilled at carving and decorating reindeer horn and this has formed the basis of a flourishing tourist attraction in the shape of souvenirs. Lapp weaving and other handicrafts are eagerly sought and purchased by visitors to the North.

Nowadays it is estimated that there are about 40,000 Lapps, and some 10,000 of these live in Sweden. However, there is no one way of really deciding if a person is a Lapp. Reindeer breeding, kinship and language are all possible ways of distinguishing Lapps, and each method yields a different total. In 1980 only about 600 households, with about 2,500 people, were directly engaged in reindeer breeding, or were completely or partially dependent on the reindeer for their livelihood.

Most Lapps earn their living in other ways and they are found working in various occupations, both in Lapp territory and in other parts of Sweden. Fishing, mining and forestry are among the most common of them.

There are two different types of reindeer breeding. In one case the animals are limited to a very large, often wooded, area. But in the other, they roam over great distances in the mountains. Then the nomadic Lapps follow them with their tents of reindeer skin, or they build a more permanent home using turf for the walls; both are called *kåta*; the ground is lined with small birch branches and covered with furs or skins, and the smoke from the fire in the middle of the floor finds its way out through a hole at the top of the cone-shaped structure.

Colourful clothes are part of the Lapp tradition – so are the reindeer. As in this picture, the two are very often seen together!

Lapp children have the choice of attending either normal schools or one of the eight special nomad schools. In the latter, the Lappish culture and language are also taught. The youngsters are keeping alive the ancient traditions and there are still many Lapps to be seen dressed in their colourfully

Rounding up the reindeer. Nowadays the deer are mostly driven by men riding on snow scooters

decorated clothes, with the dark blue woven tunics adorned with bright red and yellow braid. The primitive songs of the Lapps, rendered in a unique manner called yoiking, are still very much in use. Yet, in spite of all these efforts, there are very few young Lapps now who wish to live the life of a nomad. The reindeer herds are kept under observation from helicopters. The Lapp has his motorised snow-scooter and his walkie-talkie, and he lives in a modern house.

Nowadays it is the demand for the meat of the reindeer, transported by trucks to the South, which is the driving force that keeps alive the remnants of this romantic way of life. There are still about a quarter of a million reindeer in Sweden.

The Land of the Middle Way

Sweden has been called the Land of the Middle Way. This name is used because the country seems to have found a balance between government control and free enterprise. But Sweden may also be thought of as the Land of the Middle Way because of her foreign policy.

Sweden's foreign policy can best be described as one of neutrality. The aim of the country is to contribute to the preservation of peace. Sweden does not take sides by signing pacts with other lands. This policy of not committing the country to loyalty to a particular bloc of nations has grown up over more than one and a half centuries of peaceful, democratic development. Sweden has not been at war since 1814.

The principle of neutrality, however, does not mean that Sweden has no common ground with the aims and ideals of other more powerful nations. In fact, Sweden is strongly rooted in the democratic ideals of the western world. Being neutral does not mean that Sweden has no opinions. She has, and she expresses them. She often voices her point of view, as a neutral state, and presents her ideas on matters of world-wide importance. This is particularly so when there are strong feelings amongst the Swedish people. The Swedish Government has often expressed views on such matters as the war in Vietnam and the racial problems in South Africa. This has earned for the country the title of "Conscience of the World".

Although Sweden is itself only a small nation, there has been a growing tendency for the country to be recognised as the champion of the underdog.

Sweden has been a member of the United Nations since 1946. In this, she differs from the other traditionally neutral nation, Switzerland. Sweden has played an active role in the U.N., particularly in disarmament talks and by providing mediators, observers and troops for peace-keeping operations. In Sweden an armed unit stands in readiness for immediate action under U.N. command; in the past it has served in Korea, Kashmir, Lebanon, on the former Israeli-UAR border, in the Congo and Cyprus.

Dag Hammarskjöld, the popular and successful General Secretary of the United Nations Organisation, between 1953 and 1961, was a Swede. He was killed whilst travelling on a special peace-making journey on behalf of the U.N.

There is very strong co-operation between the Nordic countries, particularly in the fields of economics, social welfare and culture. Other Nordic nations are members in N.A.T.O.—the North Atlantic Treaty Organisation. Sweden's policy of neutrality and non-alignment prevent her from joining N.A.T.O. But this does not stop the Nordic countries from working together to solve their joint security problems.

In 1959, Sweden was one of the seven countries which founded E.F.T.A.—the European Free Trade Area. For the time being, Sweden has chosen to sign only a free trade agreement with Common Market countries, since her policy of neutrality and non-participation in pacts is felt to exclude the possibility of either full membership or association.

An increased Swedish interest in international questions has led to strong support for economic help to the developing nations, especially those in Africa. Sweden's aim has been to raise 1% of the Gross National Product for international development assistance, and the target was attained for the first time in 1975. Since 1975 this target has been largely maintained, although it did drop to only 0·93% in 1984.

The Swedes feel that the existing foreign policy makes it necessary for the nation to have a strong defence system of its own. About four times as much money is spent on defence as is given in aid to help developing nations. The country's defence is based entirely on its own finances. It is a large country to defend, with only a small population. The total coast-line is almost 2,000 kilometres (about 1,240 miles). The Swedish-Norwegian border stretches for 1,640 kilometres (over 1,000 miles), and that with Finland, in the north-east, is 536 kilometres (335 miles).

Sweden has compulsory military service for all men between 18 and 47 years of age. A period of basic training, lasting nearly a year, is followed by refresher courses and manoeuvres. The armed forces consist of army, navy and air services with a total strength exceeding 850,000 men. The air force, in particular, is very modern and well equipped. It compares favourably with that of many much larger nations. All the services have underground installations blasted out of the rock, and many of these give protection from nuclear radiation. Part of Sweden's building programme, for several years, has required the construction of large public buildings to include deep cellars which can be used as shelters in the event of a bomb-attack on the country.

The modern heart of the city of Stockholm

Sweden's efforts towards making the world a more peaceful place and a safer place for all nations, can also be seen in the active and leading part she has played in making people aware of the world-wide problems of pollution. Although Sweden herself is blessed with vast areas over which the air is remarkably clear, and there are plentiful supplies of pure water, there is a real concentration on the problems of pollution. Northern Sweden has been called the world's "Most Civilized Wilderness".

Sweden's efforts to cope with the spoiling of her lakes have shown signs of yielding good results. Strict controls are placed on the disposal of industrial waste and the use of pesticides by farmers and foresters. The fouling of the coast-lines is not only caused by the Swedes themselves, and the pollution in the air is often proved to have come from large industrial areas in countries far away. Sweden is, thus, not only keen to put her own country in order, but has already done a great deal to promote world-wide concern. The first international conference to tackle these common problems of the environment was held in Stockholm.

It is not only physical pollution which needs to be kept under control. Noise may cause stress, both at home and at work. Exposure to high levels of noise can result in injury. For many years Swedish law has required employers to provide ear protectors for workers exposed to these dangers. Aircraft noise is another big problem. Flights by supersonic planes over Swedish territory are banned.

In attempting to provide people with a better country, and world, in which to live, it is necessary to have laws and regulations. The Swedes have, for a long time, been most careful to try to protect the rights of the citizen too. As long ago as 1809, men were appointed to watch and restrict the acts of government officials and administration. The Swedish name given to this position was *Ombudsman,* and both the name and tasks connected with it have since been used in many other lands.

Of course, no country can be perfect. But a recent visitor to Sweden summed up his impressions in this way: "Many things are good, and others are not so good.....but the Swedes are making an attempt to improve things and their efforts, even when they fail, are well meant".

Index